My Top 20 Training Tips!

ISBN: 978-1-105-80662-9

Bio:

Pamela Tyree Griffin's business background is in insurance and includes stints as a Unit Manager, Claims Operations Manager, Fraud Investigator and Senior National Trainer. It was in her national training role that she realized she loved to present and teach.

She specializes in providing customized presentations with "NEWS YOU CAN USE... NOW!" Topics include Customer Service, Leadership/Management, Creative Writing, Honing Your Humor and Train the Trainer sessions.

Association of Training and she has earned the Association of Training and Development (ASTD) Certificate in E-Learning Instructional Design. She has also earned a certificate in Customer Service Management from the American Management Association.

Drawing upon her own extensive business experience, Pamela Tyree Griffin has successfully presented for Keene State College, the Massachusetts Restaurant Association, The National High School Journalism Convention, The Property Loss Research Bureau and the Connecticut Management Advisory Council, among others.

She is an internationally published writer both online and in print. She's also published two award winning, online literary magazines: "The Shine Journal" and "joyful!" She is also a certified Hospice Volunteer.

Hello!

I'm glad you have decided to pick up this little book. It came about, as much as I hate to admit it, from mistakes I've made (or have seen) on my training/presentation and audience journey.

Some of these ideas may be new to you while others-well not so much! I've selected the top 20 things I've personally messed up or observed. The solutions have worked for me and for others. Your mileage may vary.

Although each tip is numbered, there is no table of contents so it really doesn't matter where you start. There is also space for your own thoughts.

Whether you present a lot or a little, this book can help you. If you find just one tip useful – then it's worth it…at least that's my hope.

Feel free to contact me at Pamela.tyreegriffin@gmail.com.

Best,

Pamela

Tip #1: Always Start On Time!

"Time is the longest distance between two places." Tennessee Williams

Why Is This Tip Important?

Picture this: You arrive at a meeting, either in person or on the phone, and the leader says: "We'll get started in just a minute…looks like we're waiting for a few more people…" How does that make you feel? Despite everything, you managed to arrive on time. Why should you have to wait?

Starting on time is respectful to all parties. Those who arrive on time get the information on time. If you wait for late comers, it minimizes the importance of the presentation and rewards them for coming late. I make it my business to start on time - every time.

Apply The Tip:

As the leader, you set the tone for the meeting so always start on time. State the time and stick to it. It doesn't matter whether you are at the start of the day or after a break-BEGIN. Only if the room is completely empty should you deviate. If there are only one or two people still - BEGIN.

After you begin and other folks come in, do not review what has transpired in those few minutes. Keep on keeping on!

Set an odd time for the start of the meeting after a break. Instead of having people enter the room at 9:00am, for example, make the time 9:07 or 8:56, It doesn't matter so long as it's not on the hour. This tends to make people pay closer attention to the time.

Have you ever been told to imagine people naked as a way to relax before you speak? That's what my next tip is all about.

Tip #2: Imagine People Naked

"Despair is most often the offspring of ill-preparedness" Don Williams, Jr

Why Is This Tip Important?

It isn't. Imagining your audience without clothes is supposed make you relax. As a result you will often hear this "bare" advice. But I say do NOT do it. This has never worked to settle my nerves. By the looks of some folks fully clothed, I can't think they look much better naked. This advice is just plain wrong.

Apply The Tip:

If you're nervous about speaking in front of people-you are not alone .One of the best ways to eliminate anxiety is to be prepared. Know your material. Eat it. breathe it and, of course, speak it. Speak it in front of a mirror and see yourself as others see you. Record yourself and hear yourself as others hear you. The more you refine your presentation, the better it will be. Preparation is the key –well one of the keys to help alleviate your stress.

.

Now that you've learned about undressing, check out Tip#3 which is about keeping your clothes on!

Tip #3: Dress To Impress (Nana)!

"You never get a second chance to make a first impression" Unknown

Why Is This Tip Important?

It's vitally important that you look your very best for your audience it shows them that you take the meeting and the participants seriously!. Mileage varies among people: Some say we should dress extremely well, while others say dress slightly better than your audience. I don't know what either of those might look like. I do know how I would dress were I going out with my Nana. I try to look nice (but with a professional touch.)

Apply The Tip:

Dress nicely and comfortably. Try on what you plan to wear beforehand. And check out all angles, from head to toe. Look, a brand new pair of shoes is NOT what to wear for an engagement. Ladies, there's nothing wrong with wearing pants. Guys, you might also want to wear pants depending on the impression you want to make. Never equate dressing nice with over dressing. Use the Nana rule and you can't go wrong.

Now that you've finished this, you are ready to get my tip on how to properly use PowerPoint™. Tip#4: A Point About Power is next!

Tip #4: A Point About Power

"Power corrupts, PowerPoint™ corrupts absolutely." Edward Tufte

Why Is This Tip Important?

More and more, people rely on PowerPoint™ presentations. We all know the scenario: Slide after slide magically appears as if by magic. The audience sits back as the PowerPoint ™ wizard (the presenter) READS what is on every, single slide. The guy next to you is falling asleep and you are texting. You don't need to pay attention-all of the slides have been printed out and handed to you. PowerPoint™ is designed to enhance your presentation-it is NOT your presentation.

Apply The Tip:

PowerPoint™ is a grand tool and you can create some compelling presentations with it. But if you get only one thing from this book let it be this: DO NOT READ POWERPOINT™ SLIDES OUT LOUD. POWERPOINT is part of your presentation but it should not BE your presentation!

One more thing: If you must kill trees to print out your presentation, then hold your papers until afterwards. This way nobody will get ahead of you and no one will be reading it while you are trying to present it.

Now that you've finished this, you're ready to get my tip #5 on how to share your story!

TIP #5: Share Your Story

"The purpose of a storyteller is not to tell you how to think, but to give you questions to think upon." Brandon Sanderson

Why Is This Tip Important?

One of the things that can make your presentation more interesting is to share a story. If the story is something you have experienced, all the better. It helps you and your audience relate to one another. It can make your presentation more interesting.

Apply The Tip:

As you prepare your presentation, think about what has happened in your life that you might use as an example of your point. There are many stories to which people can relate. By sharing an appropriate story you are really saying,

"I know what you've been through because I've been there too!" OR you are saying," Here is an illustration of what I mean." Stories are a sure way to make your point by sharing.

One thing I recommend to people is to keep their ears and eyes open. Sometimes it's your own personal story and other times it may be something you have seen on the news. As long as the subject matter makes sense, is inoffensive and connects-weave it into your presentation.

I have even used fairy tales. I used Goldilocks and The Three Bears, to discuss ill-fitting training and how to make sure you can get it "Just right!"

Now that you're thinking of all the stories you have heard or told, how about learning my Tip #6 on the Meet and Greet!

TIP #6: Meet And Greet

"Experiment! Meet new people. That's better than any college education . . ." Amelia Earhart

Why Is This Tip Important?

We've all heard about the "Meet and Greet" and we envision all sorts of encounters with strangers. And none of it's very pretty is it? Meeting new people can overwhelm you but it doesn't have to if you know the secret. Meeting new people in the setting of your presentation is one of the easiest things you can do. Why? It's easy because you set the scene and you are in control. You OWN the room. And you might make some friends in the process.

Apply The Tip:

When you enter the room you see all kinds of people who have presumably come to see and hear you. Right away that's a positive. Think about it as you begin to approach people. Introduce yourself to the first person you come to. Ask them what they hope to get out of the meeting or what brings them there. What you want to do is get your participants talking about themselves. As you converse, you may find some commonality (kids, work, cars) and before you know it, you have an ally in the room. When you take the stage, look especially for those with whom you have connected-they are probably smiling and you are suddenly at ease.

Are you considering using jokes in your speech? Read Tip #7 before you do!

Tip #7: JOKES? Yeah…NO!

"For every ten jokes you acquire a hundred enemies." Laurence Sterne

Why Is This Tip Important?

Jokes are a most sketchy topic. Although you may have met and greeted your audience or have otherwise become acquainted, you don't know them at their core. Because of this, jokes which may be absolutely hilarious to one person may be particularly offensive to another. And you may never know this has occurred unless you count those folks beating feet to the door.

Apply The Tip:

There is a difference between a joke and general humor. The former can offend without your being aware of it while the latter may just be an innate part of who you are. Injecting a bit of humor into your presentation can create an enjoyable environment where everyone is comfortable.

Humor that pokes fun at YOU is alright. Humor that pokes fun at others may not be. If you are the least bit concerned about how you will be perceived, err on the side of not being perceived badly.

If you tell a joke, keep it relevant, clean and short or don't bother!

Stay tuned for Tip# 8: Why apologizing is not a great idea.

Tip #8: Don't Apologize!

"Never make a defense or an apology until you are accused." King Charles I

Why Is This Tip Important?

You are the expert. Your audience expects you to be prepared. The beauty of what you do and say is entirely up to you. If you skip something or forget a point, they will not know. If you APOLOGIZE, YOU DON'T INSPIRE CONFIDENCE. Your audience begins to wonder what else you've flubbed.

Apply The Tip:

This is really easy! If you make a mistake KEEP GOING! Don't refer to it, don't mention it and don't apologize for it. Just continue with your presentation and try not to forget it the next time.

Ready for Tip #9? If you want to know how to use others' work correctly you can't miss it.

Tip# 9: Give Credit Where It's Due!

"Giving credit where credit is due is a very rewarding habit to form. Its rewards are inestimable." Loretta Young

Why Is This Tip Important?

It's just plain good manners to not steal don't you think? When you take someone's words or work, you are doing just that. Putting your name on someone's else's things is just plain wrong.

Giving credit where's it's due shows respect and fairness to those involved. If the shoe was on the other foot, you would want the same.

It hit home with me once when, as one of four people working on a project, my contribution was not mentioned during the presentation. I never forgot how that made me feel.

Apply The Tip:

When you use a quote, a picture, photo or anything that you did not personally create make sure you give credit to the originator. If you create something with someone else-make sure their names appear on the work as well.

If you are paying attention, you have seen the quotes I'm using-I indicate the author-dead or alive. It's the right thing to do.

Tip#10: You May Be Quiet But Your Body Is ALWAYS Talking!

"I speak two languages, Body and English." Mae West

Why Is This Tip Important?

80-90% of all language is unspoken. It is almost universally understood. You know immediately, before one word is spoken, what someone is thinking. Their body language will tell you better and more honestly than the spoken word.

Apply The Tip:

Be aware of how you position your body. When speaking and your arms are crossed, you give a closed and unapproachable impression. When calling on or responding to people in the audience don't point. Gesture with an open palm directed toward the person. Again, it appears and is a more open position. It tells your participants that you welcome them and are open to what they have to share.

Tip #11: Tell your audience where you are going!

"A good plan is like a road map: it shows the final destination and usually the best way to get there." H. Stanley Judd

Why Is This Tip Important?

Your mileage may vary, but if you don't know where you're going, you will arrive there sooner or later. If you want to be respected as a presenter, do your homework. Your presentation needs a clear beginning, middle and end; people need to be able to follow where you are leading. The only way to lead your audience correctly is to make sure you are prepared to prepare them.

Apply The Tip:

You should state what you hope to accomplish and the ways and methods you will use to guarantee your "arrival". When opening your program, one of the first things to do is tell people what they will gain from the program. It's famously called "WIIFM" or "What's in it for me?"

If your audience can't see the benefits from what you offer, you will lose them before you begin. Think of this, not just as a tip, but also a tRip for which you'll need a map for everyone traveling with you!.

Your projector stops working! Now what? For help, check out tip #12!

Tip#12: Have A Plan B AND C!

"A good plan is like a road map: it shows the final destination and usually the best way to get there." H. Stanley Judd

Why Is This Tip Important?

Something can (and will) go wrong with your presentation-The projector won't work, the handouts don't arrive or the room isn't ready. You have a choice of either throwing up your hands and giving up or positioning yourself to succeed regardless. If you have planned well, you have "expected the unexpected"! You have a backup plan ready to go and your have a (seemingly) flawless engagement ahead of you.

Apply The Tip:

When putting your presentation together, think about what has gone wrong in the past and what could go wrong on and plan accordingly. Because good presenters don't rely totally on PowerPoint ™, they can proceed if it should fail. They have practiced their program and can move along as if the PP was never part of the thing to begin with! Good presenters remember that handouts are "nice to haves" and not necessarily "need to haves" and offer to email material to participants-while also saving the trees.

My personal experience taught me this the hard way. Some years ago I planned an entire program with every single thing on a PP. The machine died and so did I.

Make a list of what you plan to do and a list of what you will do if Plan A (or Plan B) doesn't work. You'll be glad you did!

Tip #13: MOVE!

"Life is like riding a bicycle. To keep your balance you must keep moving."

Albert Einstein

Why Is This Tip Important?

When water stands still is becomes stagnant and, well to put it nicely, rather yucky! This tip is meant not only literally but figuratively as well. Standing still when on the stage creates boredom. Even better: Stand behind the podium AND read from a piece of paper. How's that working for you?

Apply The Tip:

Move around on stage – it keeps you alive and your audience awake. As well, don't become complacent. Work hard to keep your work fresh by learning new techniques, improving your vocabulary or different ways of doing things. Any time you think you can't learn anything else-you are (or should) position to do just that! You will have a more enjoyable experience and so will your clients!

Tip# 14 will help you deal with a rowdy participant.

Tip# 14: Don't Tolerate Bad Behavior

"Bore, n.: A person who talks when you wish him to listen." Ambrose Bierce

Why Is This Tip Important?

A disruptive meeting is one of the worst things that can happen but can also be one of the best. Why? Because it demonstrates to all concerned how deftly you can handle a difficult situation. Dealing with the offending party can be done effectively, if not always as quickly as you might like.

Apply The Tip:

Someone in the audience begins to act badly-yelling, walking around, talking on the cell or otherwise being a grown up behaving badly.

You may:

Ignore the person –this has little value since it will not stop them.

Call for a break and take the person aside. When you speak with them, you say-“I realize you have some questions- let’s discuss them now.” Or better yet, “What seems to be the problem?” (and go from there.) Or best: “I see you know all about these topics-perhaps it would be best if you leave now.

Put them on the spot – Call them out and ask what they have to add specifically to the discussion-since it’s clear they do.

Call them out and ask them to leave

Give them a task!

Stop the meeting – momentarily or request a brief break.

The main thing is to not allow this person to take over your meeting or intimidate you.

Tip # 15: Setting The Stage

"All the world is a stage…"
Shakespeare

Why Is This Tip Important?

Depending on the type of meeting you have planned, the setup of your tables, chairs, etc., makes a difference. You have to consider the size of the room, the number of people and how they will see your presentation when formulating it. It matters.

Apply The Tip:

If you want to enable group participation, often a horseshoe shaped setup works well. The problem with it is that you may be limited to a very small group of 20-25 people.

Banquet style seating, while it can encourage conversation and group work, it may present problems as not everyone may be able to see everything plus-folks may be eating throughout your presentation.

Setting up separate tables in a classroom style is good if you are just speaking and people are taking notes. However, it may present problems if you want all participants to work together.

Often you won't have a say in the room setup, so take the time to actually get to know the room. This way you will be able to give the best presentation to and for your participants.

Tip #16 coming up-it's all about handwriting!

Tip # 16: Handwriting or Hieroglyphics?

"The handwriting is on the wall..."
Unknown

Why Is This Tip Important?

Before you flip out over your flip charts- make sure you remember three things:

1. Your writing is legible.
2. Your writing is legible.
3. Your writing is legible.

If nobody can read your document, what good is it?

Apply The Tip:

If you have problems writing in a straight line here is a trick:

Draw penciled lines on the blank flipchart paper. Only you will be able to see them, and it will ensure your writing is in a straight line.

Instead of the flipchart, create your presentation and then show it on a projector. Your writing will be able to be seen and read by your participants.

Colors affect people in various ways, for example:

Red: Danger

Blue: Calmness

Dark Green: Health

White: purity

Black: Death

Too much color is a bad as not enough. Study colors so that you create flipcharts which will go easy on the eyes and minds of your audience.

Consider using handouts to demonstrate your points-people will see your work and will be able to take notes as well.

Do you provide your participants with facts and figures? Tip #17 offers insight on that.

Tip #17: Why Facts Matter!

"Get the facts first. You can distort them later." Mark Twain

Why This Tip Is Important:

Whenever you take on presenting, facilitating or just trying to get your thoughts across, it's always a good idea to support your ideas with facts. People like to know that what they are learning has value beyond the room in which you are presenting.

We all like to know that we are learning something of value which has a basis in facts. From my experience, I like to hear the basis for what I'm being taught. I like to know where I can find additional information. You are probably the same way.

Apply the Tip:

People are spending something more valuable than money when they attend a seminar. They are spending something they can't ever get back - their time. Make it worth their while by providing as much background, verification and information about your topic as you can. This makes you a credible presenter and audiences appreciate that.

The next tip, #18 focuses on playing nice in the sandbox!

Tip# 18: Collaborate

"Alone we can do so little; together we can do so much." Helen Keller

Why This Tip Is important:

Whether you are a one person training department or you are one of several, it's important not to work in a vacuum. Without the input of others' points of view, you may miss an opportunity you never knew existed. You may think that because you're a seasoned facilitator, you know all you need to know. You don't. And if you say you don't know anyone with whom to work. You do…

Apply The Tip:

Get in the habit of bouncing your ideas off others. Join a professional organization. Work with others on a project. Take a course.

This doesn't mean you shouldn't work alone because sometimes that's what the situation calls for. I'm saying don't be lulled into thinking you can't learn something new or learn from someone else. After all "it's by teaching that we learn". (My mom has said that to me but I don't think it's her original saying-good words just the same.)

Collaboration builds relationships and vice versa.

Tip#19: Understanding ADDIE

"Failing to plan is planning to fail"
Unknown

Why This Tip Is Important:

ADDIE is an acronym for the method by which most instructional designers create training. It breaks down as follows:

1. Analysis
2. Design
3. Development
4. Implementation
5. Evaluation

Apply The Tip:

When creating training, you should use ADDIE or some other time tested process. By applying the five "tools" you will be sure not to leave out the important aspects of the work. In addition, this is where collaboration with subject matter experts (SMEs) or other stakeholders.

Analysis: Determine what training is needed by understanding the audience, skill gaps and what training has gone on before. You have to know that the issue is one of training and not some other problem.

Next you'll want to figure out how the training will get to the end user. Face to face, one on one, group, webinar, etc.?

Putting it all together is the next step and may include a phase of testing, review and refinement.

Now you'll roll out the training and lastly you will need to measure the training. In other words, how will you know the training has been successful?.

Tip #20: Using Activities

"Tell me and I forget. Teach me and I remember. Involve me and I learn." –variously attributed to Benjamin Franklin and Stephen Covey

Why This Tip Is Important:

People learn in many different ways. Some people learn by hearing while others retain information by seeing it. Still others like to work with their hands. There are several books and websites devoted to activities, role plays, icebreakers, etc. The challenge for you will be to select the correct activity that will underscore what you are trying to impart to your group.

Apply The Tip!

When selecting, among things to consider will be how many people will be there, what time of day you will begin and how much time you will have to execute and debrief.

Activities may be used to invigorate a tired group, add some hands on tasks to apply what's being taught or simply just to have fun.

Hi again,

We've reached the end of this particular journey and I thank you for coming along. I hope you found at least one tip that helped you.

I love to hear from folks. I can be found on Facebook and LinkedIn. As well, my email is Pamela.tyreegiffin@gmail.com. I hope to hear from you!

Best,

Pamela Tyree Griffin

PS. Be On the lookout for my next book: "My Down and Dirty 30-A Month's Worth of Training Tips" It's also for the good of all mankind!

www.ingramcontent.com/pod-product-compliance
Ingram Content Group UK Ltd.
Pitfield, Milton Keynes, MK11 3LW, UK
UKHW020216250726
13967UKWH00001B/16

9 781105 806629